Contents

1	Welcome to Planet Football!	2
2	Colours and characters	4
3	World Cup shock	6
4	Sensational stadiums	8
5	Freezing football	10
6	Goal of the Century	12
7	Japan's joy	16
8	Pitch invaders	18
9	Denmark calling	20
10	Funny old game	22
11	Teranga tales	24
12	Football futures	26
13	Football glory	28
	Footballing greats	30

Written by Simon Mugford

Collins

1 Welcome to Planet Football!

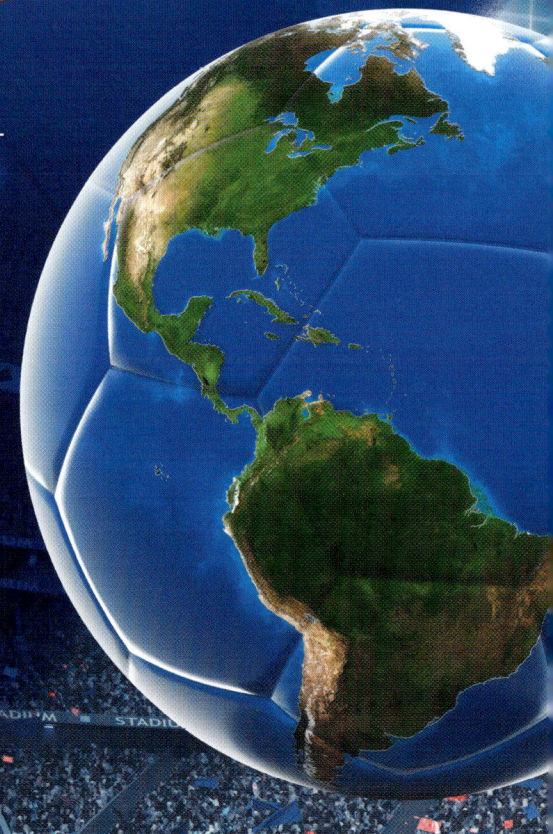

Football is the world's biggest sport. It's played – and watched – in every corner of the globe, from gardens and playgrounds to stadiums packed with thousands of cheering supporters.

From surprising and funny moments, to stories of the greatest footballers in history, this is … Planet Football.

KNOW THE SCORE

The 2022 men's World Cup Final was watched by 1.5 billion people on television, which is around 18% of the world's population!

2 Colours and characters

Wearing the colours of your favourite team is a great way to show your support. For some fans, the bigger and brighter their outfit is, the better!

Dutch fans created a sea of orange at the 2006 World Cup in Germany.

Teams often have a mascot – usually an animal – and someone wears a costume of the animal at matches.

These football mascots are racing to raise money for charity!

3 World cup shock

At the 2022 men's World Cup, Argentina lost their first match 2-1 against Saudi Arabia. This shocked football fans because it was only the fourth time that Saudi Arabia had won a World Cup match, and Argentina had already been crowned World Cup winners twice!

However, after this match, Argentina went on to win the World Cup for the third time.

Saudi Arabia players celebrate their famous win.

FOOTBALL ICONS
Lionel Messi

Country: Argentina

Messi's unrivalled ball skills and goal-scoring feats won him the Ballon d'Or (world's best player award) a record eight times in 14 years.

In 2022, he achieved his dream when his team won the World Cup.

4 Sensational stadiums

Each team is based at their local football stadium. There are high-tech wonders …

… like Real Madrid's Bernabéu, where the roof can be closed and the pitch moved underground for different events …

… while some stadiums are in spectacular locations, like Henningsvaer in Norway.

KNOW THE SCORE

The largest football crowd in history was at the 1950 World Cup, where 173,850 fans watched Uruguay beat Brazil 2-1 at the Maracana Stadium in Rio de Janeiro.

5 Freezing football

At the IceSnow Football tournament in Switzerland, football is played on an ice rink covered in snow. Players wear special boots (and gloves!) in this chilly version of the game.

IceSnow football is perfect for a sliding tackle!

FOOTBALL ICONS
Pelé

Country: Brazil

Pelé became an international sensation when, aged **17**, he scored a hat-trick (three goals in the same match) in the **1958** World Cup semi-final. He went on to win the competition three times in **14** years.

6 Goal of the Century

In 1986, Diego Maradona was the greatest football player in the world. In that year's World Cup quarter-final against England, he scored two goals. For the first goal, he used his hand – an illegal move which the referee didn't see! However, Maradona then ran with the ball past four England players – and the goalkeeper – to score what's been called the "Goal of the Century".

Maradona on his way to score the "Goal of the Century"

Maradona lifts the World Cup in 1986.

Next goal wins

In 2001, American Samoa were beaten 31–0 by Australia in a World Cup qualifier – the worst defeat in international football.

American Samoa goalkeeper Nicky Salapu watches the ball go past him – again!

KNOW THE SCORE

Only around 45,000 people live in American Samoa, compared to around 26 million in Australia, so it was much harder to find a team of good footballers!

Football icons
Johan Cruyff

Country: Netherlands

In the 1970s, Cruyff was famous for playing "Total Football", a style of passing and movement that led to the way the game is played today. He won the Ballon d'Or three times in 14 years.

7 Japan's joy

In 2011, Japan played in the Women's World Cup just a few months after a terrible earthquake hit their country. Despite not being able to practise for the tournament, they played brilliantly – beating favourites the USA – to lift the trophy.

Japan became winners at a very difficult time for their country.

FOOTBALL ICONS
Homare Sawa

Country: Japan

Sawa captained Japan to their famous World Cup win in 2011 and was the star of the competition – scoring the most goals and being voted as the tournament's best player.

8 Pitch invaders

Sometimes, an unexpected guest turns up at a match! In 2024, a raccoon ran onto the pitch during a game in the USA between Philadelphia Union and NYCFC.

Match officials in England had to deal with a chicken on the pitch during a match between Blackburn Rovers and Burnley in 2014!

9 Denmark calling

Denmark didn't qualify for the 1992 European Championships, but when Yugoslavia had to withdraw, Denmark took their place. Incredibly, these last-minute entrants went on to win the tournament!

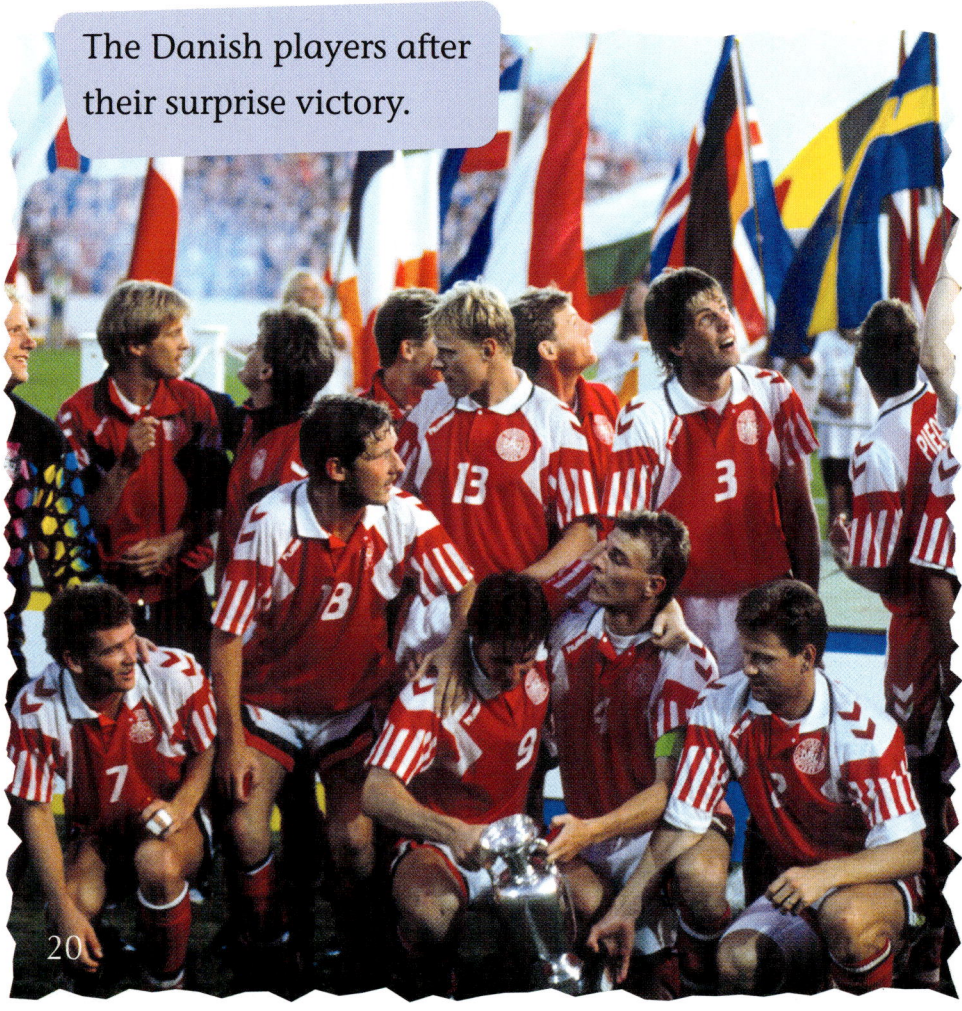

The Danish players after their surprise victory.

FOOTBALL ICONS
Lily Parr

Country: England

Lily Parr was one of the first stars of women's football. Parr started in 1920 and played for more than 30 years for the Dick, Kerr Ladies team, scoring around 1,000 goals.

10 Funny old game

One of the strangest goals in the English Premier League came in 2009, when the ball bounced off a beach ball that had been thrown onto the pitch – and into the goal!

The striker scored – with help from the beach ball!

Colombia's goalkeeper René Higuita cleared the ball with an unusual backwards overhead kick, in a match against England in 1995.

René Higuita performs his "scorpion kick".

11 Teranga tales

Egypt and Cameroon have dominated the Africa Cup of Nations, winning the tournament 12 times between them. So, when Senegal won for the first time in 2021, it was a historical moment.

Senegal – the "Lions of Teranga" – celebrate their victory.

FOOTBALL ICONS
Marta

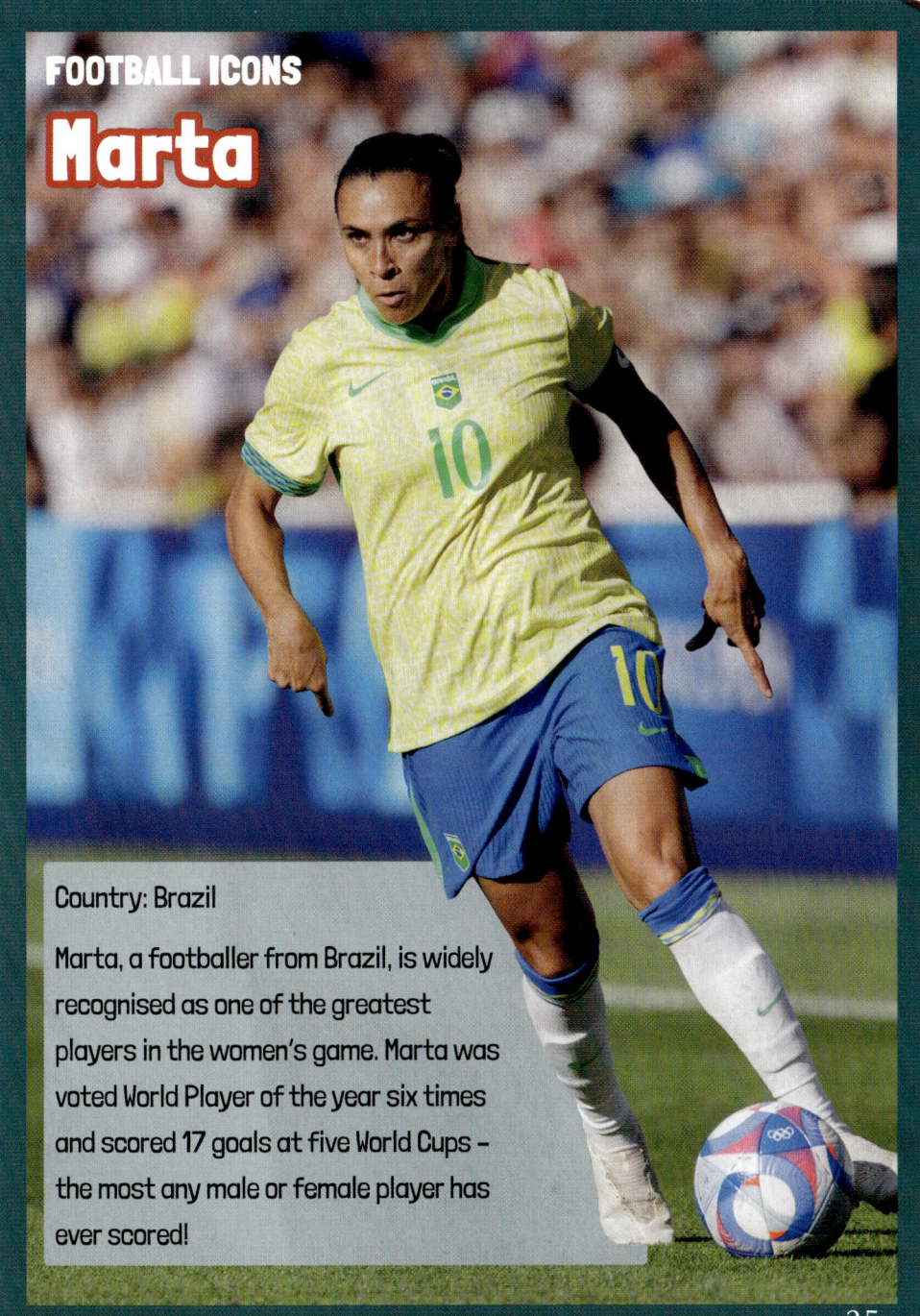

Country: Brazil

Marta, a footballer from Brazil, is widely recognised as one of the greatest players in the women's game. Marta was voted World Player of the year six times and scored 17 goals at five World Cups – the most any male or female player has ever scored!

12 Football futures

The "players" at the Robot World Cup improve each year, but they are very slow and often fall over!

Human footballers' jobs are probably safe – for now!

Professional video gamers play football matches, too. There's even a World Cup!

In this FIFA esports competition for pro gamers, Real Madrid are playing … Real Madrid!

KNOW THE SCORE

The first competitive match to use VAR (a referee who uses video to check decisions) was a Dutch Cup match between Ajax and Willem II in 2016.

13 Football glory

An important win for a football team can spark huge celebrations. In 2024, Bayer Leverkusen won the Bundesliga (the top German football league) for the first time in its history. They did it without losing a match in the league for the whole season!

Bayer Leverkusen fans celebrate on the pitch.

Players who score lots of goals often become famous for their way of celebrating.

Australian striker Sam Kerr celebrates her goal with a backflip.

Football continues to entertain and surprise, making the fans sing, shout, cheer, laugh and sometimes cry, wherever they are in the world.

Will you be watching?

Footballing greats

Most Best Player Awards

Lionel Messi
The Argentinean star won the Ballon d'Or eight times.

Record Football Crowd

Uruguay versus Brazil, 1950
173,850 fans watched this World Cup match.

Biggest International Defeat

American Samoa
The tiny island nation lost 31–0 to Australia in 2001.

Most World Cup Goals

Marta
The Brazilian legend scored 17 times in five tournaments.

Biggest Shock

Denmark, 1992 European Championships
The team won the tournament despite replacing Yugoslavia at the last minute.

Ideas for reading

Written by Gill Matthews
Primary Literacy Consultant

Reading objectives:
- be introduced to non-fiction books that are structured in different ways
- draw on what they already know or on background information and vocabulary provided by the teacher
- answer and ask questions

Spoken language objectives:
- ask relevant questions to extend their understanding and knowledge
- use relevant strategies to build their vocabulary
- articulate and justify answers, arguments and opinions

Curriculum links: Geography: locational knowledge

Interest words: biggest, greatest, best, largest, strangest

Build a context for reading

- Ask children to look at the front cover of the book. Read the title. Ask what they think the book is about.
- Read the back-cover blurb. Explore children's knowledge and experience of football. Ask why they think football is such a popular game.
- Point out that this is an information book. Encourage children to talk about what they know about non-fiction books.
- Ask them to find the contents page. Discuss the purpose and organisation of a contents.
- Ask children to use the contents to find Chapter 1.

Understand and apply reading strategies

- Read pp2–3 aloud. Ask children if they have watched a football match. Encourage them to expand their responses by asking further questions e.g Where was the game? Did you go to the match or watch on TV?
- Ask children to read pp4–5. Ask which teams they support and why.
- Ask children to read pp6–7 and to formulate a question relating to what they have read. They can then ask a friend or the group their question.